INVISIBLE MARKETING

INVISIBLE MARKETING

A HIDDEN TOOL FOR CONNECTING WITH CONSUMERS THROUGH LICENSING

JEFF LOTMAN

LIONCREST
PUBLISHING

INVISIBLE MARKETING

A Hidden Tool for Connecting with Consumers through Licensing

ISBN   978-1-5445-0726-2 *Hardcover*

978-1-5445-0724-8 *Paperback*

978-1-5445-0725-5 *Ebook*

This book would not have been possible without three people: my wife, Thérèse, who's always supported me in all my endeavors, and my daughters, Anna Sophia and Gianna, who've put up with a lifetime of "Do you think brand X could also be a Y?" questions.

Also, to all of you, who have to compete in this very tough, rapidly changing world—hopefully this book helps you go out there and kick some other brands' asses!

CONTENTS

Brand licensing allows us to extend our brand to groups of customers we otherwise wouldn't be able to reach. It's like a megaphone for our brand.

—HENRY FORD III

INTRODUCTION

WHAT IS INVISIBLE MARKETING?

I've heard it time and again from chief marketing officers (CMOs) and brand managers: "I don't want to do licensing—it's going to damage my brand."

Where does this hesitation come from? Why does brand licensing have such a bad reputation?

For one thing, it's a terrible name. "Licensing." You hear that word and you think about getting a fishing or a driver's license.

Here's the deal: a "license" is simply a legal document. That said, "licensing" is a misleading way to think about the industry. What we do really should be called "brand extensions": a manufacturer extends its brands to connect with new consumers.

And yet, like it or not (and to be clear, I don't), we're stuck with the term "licensing." It's not going anywhere. What matters more is that we challenge the myths and misconceptions surrounding the practice—so that folks start to understand what licensing really means and how they can wield it to create opportunity.

For example, a lot of people still think about licensing as all the logo stuff you see when you go into a store and there's a shirt with an insignia on it from some brand. That's *not* licensing. That's just label slapping.

When I hear a CMO pooh-pooh licensing, what they don't grasp is that it's simply another marketing tool, similar to the ones they've long been accustomed to (such as advertising, public relations, social media, and events). But because licensing involves *products*—all the stuff we buy, use, wear, and eat—the connection with the consumer is very close and intimate, likely more so than any other form of marketing.

"Licensing" is better than any other forms of marketing because it creates a deeper connection with your consumers.

A HIDDEN TOOL

It may surprise readers to hear me say this, but licensing is not about the money. At least primarily. That these brand extensions make money, that someone pays you for the license, is certainly critical, but it's not the only reason you should be doing this, nor is it even the biggest.

Above all, licensing is an opportunity to expand your brand and connect with new customers. That's the sweet spot of any marketing initiative.

Yet many companies fail to appreciate this truth. They don't realize the staggering amount of value and untapped potential lurking in the shadows.

Which is why I call licensing "invisible marketing."

Expand your brand and connect with new customers with invisible marketing.

Walk into a Walmart today and you'll find pallets of Hostess-branded boxes for Post cereal. There are Twinkies, Honey Bun, and Donettes. What's behind licensing deals like these? What's the hidden value for Hostess (which is a Global Icons client)?

Hostess products are typically sold in the ready-to-eat pastry aisle, alongside baked goods and sweet snacks. The products also benefit from 100 percent aided awareness: the Hostess brand is beloved and well known. Indeed, Twinkies is an icon of American snack food. So there's a lot of latent equity waiting to be unlocked and explored.

Now, for the first time, Hostess is appearing in a completely different aisle—cereal—in five thousand Walmarts[1] and other grocery stores across the country. What's that worth in dollars? A good amount, for sure. But what's it worth in terms of expanding the brand and reaching new customers (and stopping their competitors from doing the same)? That's priceless.

---

1   "Total Number of Walmart Stores in the United States from 2012 to 2019, by Type," Statista, 2020, https://www.statista.com/statistics/269425/total-number-of-walmart-stores-in-the-united-states-by-type/.

Source: © Hostess Brand & Post Consumer Brands

Source: © Hostess Brand & Post Consumer Brands

Similarly, consider Vicks, a company that's been around for ages and is known for its VapoRub. An industry friend of mine, Nancy Bailey, founder of the Nancy Bailey

Agency, was responsible for putting together the deal for a popular line of Vicks-branded electric vaporizers.

To me, this is a perfect example of a brand extension. For generations Vicks has been a trusted name when it comes to taking care of congestion and other cold symptoms. So when the new branded product came out, it couldn't have felt more natural: "Do you like our VapoRub? Well, here's another way to pacify your pain...ta-da, the Vicks Vaporizer!"

Vicks Vaporizer is the perfect example of a brand extension.

These brand extensions are one of the best ways to connect to customers—but amazingly, many companies are missing the boat.

Which is where this book comes in.

In the following chapters, you'll learn about the power of invisible marketing and how to do it, using our clear, concise method to extend your brand. You'll encounter example after example of savvy brands—maybe even some of your competitors—that have taken advantage of this hidden tool and are now reaping the benefits, while you stay stuck on the sidelines.

Isn't it about time you got in on the game too?

WHO ARE YOU?

If you're like so many of the CPG (that's "consumer packaged goods") companies I talk to, you're not breaking through to your customers to the degree you desire or believe you deserve. You're working your butt off, doing everything you think you're supposed to be doing.

Why, then, are all your inputs, all these different tools you're using, not giving you what you want? Why are so many customers still going to your competitors? Why does it seem like retailers are cutting down your market share?

What should you be doing differently? Should you increase your advertising? Double down on PR? Pursue some "experiential activations"?

No. These aren't the solutions that'll trigger the revolutionary results you're looking for.

You'll spend lots of money on media—but so will everyone else. In fact, they're spending more than $1 trillion a year (globally) to broadcast their brands. They're all buying the same TV ads, the same Facebook ads, and the same PR at the same events.

It's not that these efforts don't work. It's that they don't work as they did before. And it's becoming harder and harder to yield dividends from these levers because so many people are using them (consumers see, on average, five thousand ads per day[2]). It's like trying to push a boulder up a mountain.

Look, there was a period when you could just jump on social media and immediately start building a following and get people to visit your website. Not anymore. Now there are countless influencers going after countless niches. It's information overload.

How on earth do you compete in an environment like this? What's more, how do you create a new product in an environment like this? Not only are the costs sky-high, but the failure rate is also abysmal. Out of the thirty thousand new products created each year, 70 to 80 percent will fail.[3] It's enough to make you want to pull out your hair.

I get it. I get why you might even be compelled to leave the industry altogether.

Don't.

---

2   Oksana Tunikova, "How Many Ads Do You Actually See Daily?" *StopAd Blog*, April 6, 2018, https://stopad.io/blog/ads-seen-daily.

3   Lonny Kocina, "What Percentage of New Products Fail and Why?" *MarketSmart Newsletters*, May 3, 2017, https://www.publicity.com/marketsmart-newsletters/percentage-new-products-fail/.

Before you throw in the towel, consider this: if you want to break out and find new customers who look at your brand differently—if you want to be discovered by new people and be seen in new areas—you can. But you need to do something *different*. As the old saying goes, doing the same thing over and over and expecting a different result is the definition of insanity.

Fortunately, there *is* another path, a way out of this madness. Want new customers and new impressions and more awareness and market share? Want to sell more products? *You can.*

You can do it all through invisible marketing.

Are you licensing out, or only licensing in?

Maybe you're saying to yourself, "But wait, Jeff—I'm already doing licensing!" Okay, so you've dipped your toe into the water. But have you been licensing *out*, or are you only licensing *in*?

If you're like a lot of companies, you've dabbled in licensing, but you haven't thought to take your own brand or brands *out*. You pay money to add other brands to yours; you believe this adds value. But why aren't people paying *you* for your brand and your equity?

It's time to get real: you want your customer back. You want people to recognize that yours is the best brand. You want families to see your product differently.

Well, I'm sorry to be the bearer of bad news, but advertising's not going to cut it anymore. It's a widely quoted statistic nowadays that it takes *seven times* for an ad to stick in the mind of a consumer. Yes, in the *Mad Men* days you could advertise a pet rock and somebody would buy it. But that time is long gone. The old methods and tools are just that: old and obsolete.

So what are you going to do about it?

THIS BOOK IS NOT FOR EVERYBODY

There's an old expression in licensing: "Fortune follows fame." What does this mean? Well, first, you have to ask yourself: who are you as a brand? If you're still very young in your process and your awareness—if your brand is only in one or two stores—you're likely not ready to launch a license.

Yes, licensing is a fantastic way to make money and build your brand. But let's face it: no one knows you are you.

Be honest: is your brand ready for the big time?

For now, focus on building your core product. Then come back to licensing when you're bigger and your name has more equity. You'll still be ahead of the game, because you understand the power of invisible marketing—and others don't.

It's better to wait than to take a big risk now, even if you do succeed in getting a small deal. I know this because I've helped countless companies, of varying sizes and at varying stages in their development, and I've seen first-hand what works and what doesn't.

WHO AM I?

As the founder and chief executive of one of the largest privately held global brand-licensing agencies, I've advised many market-leading clients—including some of the most iconic brands in history, from BMW and Ford to Nokia and even the United States Postal Service.

Through it all, I've seen how a hidden tool—invisible marketing—not only adds cash value, but is also unbelievably effective in helping companies penetrate new markets and generate new business opportunities.

Simply put, invisible marketing is the best way to get customers to feel good about your brand.

Now, with the publication of my first book, I'm sharing what I've learned over the past two decades about building dynamic brand extensions.

Drawing from the stories of companies that have used licensing to unleash their brand's potential—from Wolfgang Puck to Caterpillar and Duraflame—and based on exclusive interviews with many of the leaders of those brands, I'll help you understand what licensing *is* and *isn't* and how to use it to connect to new customers in a way that's authentic and engaging.

Let's dive in.

Invisible marketing is the best way to get customers to feel good about your brand.

CHAPTER 1

THE POWER OF LICENSING

The first thing you need to know about licensing is that it's *everywhere*, all around you, wherever you shop, whether in a brick-and-mortar store, on the street, on a website, or in an app. Take out your wallet to pay for something and odds are high that what you're buying is, in fact, a licensed product. (Indeed, some credit cards are licensed.)

Licensing is a huge industry, with over $180 billion in worldwide retail sales across every retail channel (see graphs later in the chapter). Brand licensing, the area we will focus on, accounts for almost $60 billion alone!

Licensing is ubiquitous, but it goes largely unnoticed. People don't see it. They don't know that they're purchasing something licensed. This is why it is so misunderstood. It takes place behind the scenes, in the shadows.

It is also what makes licensing so *powerful*.

The best licensed products, the ones that amplify your brand the most, are precisely the ones where you're unaware of the underlying partnership. Your brand is being seen and used by the consumer without them even knowing that they're being sold to.

And, in a way, they're not. When it comes down to it, what you're really doing is filling a need. You're helping people in their lives, in whatever capacity it is that they're looking to your product for—and in whatever category *you're* trying to break into.

That's the whole premise of invisible marketing.

What makes licensing so misunderstood is also what makes it so powerful.

In the Introduction, I mentioned Vicks Vaporizer as the perfect example of an invisible success. No one even knows or pays attention to the fact that Vicks doesn't actually make the vaporizer (it's produced by a company called Kaz). All the customer sees is the name "Vicks," a trustworthy brand that's been in business for many, many years.

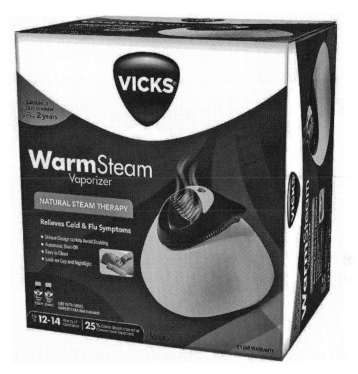

Source: © Procter & Gamble and Helen of Troy Limited

Or take Flintstones vitamins for kids. It's a licensed product that's been around seemingly since Fred and Wilma. (To be precise, these sweet supplements hit the market in the late 1960s.) Clearly, it's not the Flintstones themselves making the product. But no one thinks about that. All that matters is that the vitamins are fun and colorful and shaped like the animated Stone Age characters.

In other words, because the Flintstones brand is so beloved, its extension into multivitamin tablets has been successful and enduring.

This is not to say that every licensed product will last for fifty years. But if you do licensing *right*—if you take the advice in the coming chapters and put it into action—you too can leverage the power of this hidden tool.

You've come to this book because you want to amplify your own brand—and because the tools you've been using aren't giving you the edge you're looking for. You're curious about licensing but maybe not yet fully persuaded. Perhaps you still have some lingering concerns about damaging your brand.

But as you'll see in this chapter, enduring examples of licensing are everywhere you turn, and their effectiveness can be seen in a variety of ways, across verticals, and at every price point.

GLOBAL RETAIL SALES OF LICENSED MERCHANDISE
by Property Type 2018

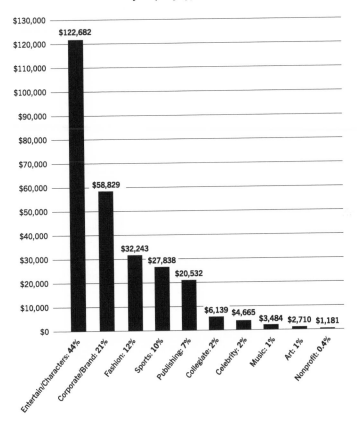

Source: Licensing International 2019 Global Licensing Survey

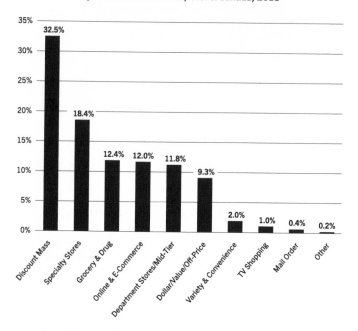

RETAIL SALES OF LICENSED MERCHANDISE
by Distribution Channel, U.S. & Canada, 2018

- Discount Mass: 32.5%
- Specialty Stores: 18.4%
- Grocery & Drug: 12.4%
- Online & E-Commerce: 12.0%
- Department Stores/Mid-Tier: 11.8%
- Dollar/Value/Off-Price: 9.3%
- Variety & Convenience: 2.0%
- TV Shopping: 1.0%
- Mail Order: 0.4%
- Other: 0.2%

Source: Licensing International 2019 Global Licensing Survey

LICENSING WILL NOT DAMAGE YOUR BRAND

California Pizza Kitchen (CPK) frozen pizza may not have been around as long as Flintstones vitamins, but when it comes to the modern era of licensing, CPK is a classic. When the product first emerged, there was a big question about whether the frozen pizzas would hurt restaurant sales. At the time, the chain was doing a brisk business in its home state of California. Would the new supermarket pies cannibalize the market for CPK's restaurants?

Quite the opposite, as it turns out.

Research showed that the licensed product helped to establish brand awareness in new markets. CPK was then able to build on that awareness to open new restaurants in those markets.

Another restaurant-chain case study is TGI Fridays. When Fridays-branded frozen products like loaded potato skins came out, sales at the chain's restaurants went up, not down. It became clear that consumers view going out for a meal and buying restaurant-branded food in a supermarket as two separate and distinct buying occasions.

In other words, people didn't say, "Oh, I'm not going to Fridays tonight; I'll stay in and eat their frozen chicken wings." Instead, they saw these two options as entirely different. When they were home, they would eat the chicken wings just as they would any other food in their freezer. And when they felt like dining out, they'd go to Fridays.

The point is, the licensed product didn't kill or even hurt the primary customer. On the contrary, the invisible hand of the licensed product pulled the brand to greater prominence—with restaurants soon expanding all over the country. In fact, the frozen products ultimately became an even bigger driver of revenue than the brick-and-mortar stores. Talk about a win-win!

Now imagine how much money, how much investment, it would have taken to build that kind of brand awareness. Invisible marketing allowed Fridays to shortcut that process and expedite its growth. The licensed product fed the success of the restaurants, and vice versa.

In the case of California Pizza Kitchen, it also helped that the market for frozen pizza at the time was rudimentary. There was really no competition back then for gourmet frozen pizza with fresh, healthy ingredients and unusual flavors like Thai chicken. People were still used to those old cardboard frozen flatbreads that you threw in your freezer and heated up when you needed a quick stomach-filler.

The myth that licensing out will hurt your existing business is just that: a myth.

I love the stories of CPK and TGI Fridays because both companies were pioneers of restaurant licensing. No one else was doing what they embarked upon in the late nineties. They proved once and for all that licensing doesn't siphon customers away from your brand's primary product. On the contrary, licensed products allow you to build your brand that much faster.

THE CREAM OF THE LICENSING CROP

Diageo, makers of Baileys Irish Cream, learned a similar lesson when they took the coffee-creamer category by storm. This was a retail space that had been around for a long time and was relatively boring. Basically, you had your nonfat and regular creamer. As for flavors, there was vanilla and not much else.

But then everything changed when the manufacturer HP Hood had the idea to secure the rights to create a Baileys-flavored coffee creamer.

People had been pouring the liqueur—Baileys Irish Cream—into their coffee for years. It was a variation on the old Irish coffee, where you put whiskey, cream, and sugar in your cup o' joe. But Baileys possessed its own unique flavor that people had grown to love. Now, HP Hood wanted to make a flavored creamer that tasted just like the rich liqueur.

The creamer would be nonalcoholic; that was a given. It *had* to be in order to get distribution nationally, because a lot of retailers can't carry alcohol. But the manufacturer, HP Hood, believed that customers would go for it just for the taste.

At first, the deal didn't seem like it was going to happen. The company that owns Baileys, Diageo, was hesitant.

Their Irish cream had been selling very well, and they knew that a lot of this success had to do with customers pouring it into their coffee to Irish-ize it. They were afraid the branded creamer would undercut their own business.

It took years for them to finally agree. But once they did, the licensed product turned out to be a huge success, becoming one of the biggest branded flavored coffee creamers on the market. As with California Pizza Kitchen pizzas, Baileys creamer ended up essentially building a whole new category. And far from denting sales of the liqueur, this extension gave it a significant lift.

A CUT ABOVE

Compared to food and alcohol, fashion brands have been heavily involved with licensing for quite a while. Licensing has traditionally been the fashion industry's bread and butter—more so than with any of the other categories we discuss in this chapter. But again, because this kind of marketing is invisible, it's not something that people are aware of. They just think the designer makes everything.

If that sounds naive to you, think again. Are *you* always aware of what's licensed and what's not? Are you consciously attuned to the fact that your Prada sunglasses aren't made by Prada? Or that Gucci doesn't make your Gucci sneakers? Or that Disney doesn't make your *Frozen* T-shirt?

> Consumers of licensed fashion products assume the designer is also the manufacturer.

The reality is that almost every fashion designer uses licensing. From their eyewear to their furniture, from Ralph Lauren to Givenchy to Fred Segal, licensing is huge in apparel.

Case in point: Calvin Klein (CK) underwear.

In the 1980s, designer jeans were all the rage, and Calvin Klein was the biggest name in the biz. Then Calvin was approached about doing underwear. While he was intrigued, this wasn't something he wanted to manufacture himself.

Younger readers may not remember this, but at the time, underwear—and particularly men's underwear—was fairly boring. Men bought it (usually under the Jockey brand) more as a necessity than a fashion statement.

But then something incredible happened. In the early nineties, with a little help from a young model nick-named Marky Mark, Calvin Klein revolutionized the fashion industry with his men's underwear. There were provocative billboards everywhere of a nearly naked Mark Wahlberg wearing nothing but his CK briefs (with Calvin's name on the waist).

The ads were highly sexual and not everyone approved. But the controversy fueled sales, and the whole thing just took off.

Source: © Phillips-Van Heusen Corporation

Ultimately, as with CPK, TGI Fridays, and Baileys, Calvin Klein took a staid category that no one really cared about, where there was nothing exciting going on, and added a brand to it. In the process, he completely transformed and dominated the space.

Men's underwear went from a utilitarian product, something you *had* to buy, to something you *wanted* to buy. Men wanted to be seen wearing certain boxers and briefs.

Yet consumers had no idea—and still don't—that CK wasn't actually making this stuff. That's the nature of invisible marketing.

Find a "boring" space and add excitement to it with your brand.

EXTENDING YOUR BRAND TO NEW CATEGORIES

I once heard someone say, "If our cars acted like our laptops do, we'd be in deep trouble." Think about how much aggravation, how many bugs and restarts, you accept from your computer. When it comes to automobiles, obviously humanity can't tolerate that kind of volatility. Cars are life or death.

I thought about that quote a lot when I was working on a licensing project with Ford.

Ford, of course, is an iconic American brand. And their

trucks are their most profitable line. The company has made a fortune because people believe that their trucks are built "Ford tough." Indeed, the reason this slogan has lasted so long is obvious: it's true. Anyone who's owned a Ford automobile knows they're engineered for the long haul.

So, when it came to extending Ford's brand to a new category, we knew the licensed product needed to retain certain basic traits. Whatever the product, it needed to be tough, durable, and reliable.

Like cars, power tools can be life or death. If you're going to grab one of these bad boys, you don't want it to break or misfire. The same goes for generators: if you're buying one for your home, you want to know for an absolute fact that it's going to start. After all, when you need it, you really friggin' need it. As NASA's Gene Kranz said, "Failure is not an option."

It's a different story with your laptop. You accept that your ThinkPad or MacBook is going to go on the fritz here and there and you'll have to reboot. But there's no reboot on an outdoor generator or power washer. These are things that just *have* to work, each and every day.

The same way that Ford trucks work each and every day.

Working with Ford as a client, we knew we needed their customers to trust these new products just as they trusted the trucks they put their lives into.

So, the first thing we did was to look at Ford's customers. We learned that the typical Ford buyer likes to work on their car, likes to tinker in their garage, and has a real love for their vehicle. How, then, could we take that experience and broaden it? How could we, and Ford, connect to more customers in their garages and work sheds?

We called the solution we devised the "man-cave strategy." What were the things that the customer would want around their car that would complement the experience? That's where the idea of creating hand tools, power tools, generators, and power washers came from.

Ultimately, not only did those new products and categories succeed in their own right, but they also cemented Ford's bond with their customers at a very close level.

Take your customers' experience—what they love—and figure out how to broaden it.

The licensed products we did for Ford were tough and durable. But again, consumers didn't think about the fact that the products weren't actually manufactured by Ford.

All they cared about was that the product was stamped with a name they recognized and respected.

As a result, the products became part of the customers' lives—just like their beloved vehicles.

MAKING PRODUCTS PART OF THE CUSTOMER'S LIFE

In this chapter, we've looked at several examples of brilliant brand licensing. In terms of distribution channels, they run the gamut: from drugs (Vicks Vaporizer, Flintstones vitamins) and grocery stores (CPK pizzas, TGI Fridays frozen products, Baileys coffee creamer) to department stores (Calvin Klein) and specialty retail (Ford).

In each of these areas, one thing stands out above all else: because of the collaboration between brand and manufacturer, the consumer *feels good* about the original brand. To be precise, the consumer feels *even better* about the original brand.

That's because products are more than just dispensable items. Products, and the brands they represent, are part and parcel of our daily lives. Again, this is the power of invisible marketing.

But it is a power that can only be unleashed when you do licensing *right*. The history of brand extensions has seen its share of cautionary tales too—and as we'll see in the next chapter, much can be learned from exploring what *didn't* work.

CHAPTER 2

THE BEST-LAID PLANS

Licensed tools for Ford was a fruitful endeavor all around: for the automaker, for their customers, and for Global Icons. It was also a great example of how to seamlessly translate a brand identity—in this case, the toughness and durability associated with trucks—into adjacent products and new categories.

But one aspect of that partnership that I haven't talked about yet is the importance of *quality*. Part of our contract negotiation with the manufacturer involved the insistence that they create the tools from scratch, as opposed to delivering ones that had been built from original-equipment-manufacturer (OEM) stock.

The point was that the products needed to be "Ford tough," just like the trucks. For Ford, this license was about far more than royalty payments. Having tools that were of superior quality was absolutely critical.

Ford knew that when you stretch, or extend, your brand in new directions, the extension has to deliver equal equity. If it doesn't, the potential reward isn't worth the risk.

Kawasaki learned this lesson the hard way. The powersports-vehicle company also got into the tool-licensing game, but, unlike Ford, they didn't create *new* tools. Instead, they used OEM products from China, changed the colors, and slapped a logo on them.

The problem wasn't the license itself. The tool idea was a good one. After all, it paid off for Ford, and it could have with Kawasaki. Rather, the issue here was quality, consistency, and equity.

To be fair, the items weren't significantly worse than what was already on the market. But compared to Kawasaki's illustrious bikes, the tools were undeniably inferior. Although the products may have been good enough and cheap enough to remain on the market—in fact, they're still sold today—the consensus among almost everybody in the tool space was that they reflected poorly on the Kawasaki brand.

When you don't put the proper equity into your licensed products, you spark a disconnect between the original product and the extension. That does great damage to your brand.

On the flip side, when you deliver equity and do it in a unique way, as Ford does, the value to your brand is enormous—and goes beyond dollars and cents.

> When you extend your brand, the extension has to deliver equal equity.

PLAYING IN A SANDBOX WHERE YOU SHOULDN'T BE

Look, it's easy to Monday-morning quarterback anything, but the truth is we all make mistakes in this licensing game. Nobody's perfect. As a matter of fact, one of our past clients, Duraflame, went into a category that seemed to make a lot of sense, but then it turned out that they couldn't win over enough customers. (Thankfully, we had successes with them later on, which we discuss in chapter 6.)

When it comes to fire logs, Duraflame is number one. They figured that since they're a heating company, they might license their brand for the fuel canisters you put underneath chafing dishes.

Unfortunately, this was a category where the brand Sterno already dominated. And when I say, "dominate," I mean *dominate*—to the tune of 90 percent market share. Sterno is the Kleenex of fuel products: people don't say "I want a can of fuel." They say "I want a can of Sterno."

Nonetheless, we all thought the category would work for Duraflame. The licensee did a great job and made a personalized product. In this case, unlike with the Kawasaki-branded tools, the equity was there. The quality was there.

But to challenge a monolith was a mistake. For example, since Sterno owned the market, retailers didn't give Duraflame any shelf space. When you're up against a monopoly, it's hard to break out.

Even when you have strong brand equity, it may not be enough to penetrate a retail-based market.

Always pay close attention to your competitors.

A BRIDGE TOO FAR

As we've seen, hindsight is twenty-twenty, and we all come into these projects with the best intentions. No one goes into a new market thinking, "How can I waste my money and hurt my consumer?" But the more you can study the industry and learn from the challenges that others have faced, the better equipped you'll be.

Sometimes, even if the quality is outstanding, as with Duraflame, the licensed product just doesn't break through. In that case, the problem was the competition.

But often the impasse has to do more with the new category itself.

For example, everyone knows Johnnie Walker. It's a premium scotch, and the company's brand team only wanted to do things that are premium. So they made the decision to launch a premium line of menswear—a drinking suit—in Japan.

This idea wasn't as out there as it may seem. Brands often try things overseas that they wouldn't do in their own territory because they're afraid to get it wrong. Plus, Johnnie Walker is big in Asia.

So how did things work out?

The end product was indeed nice. It looked good. The quality was outstanding. They made it with great features. But it didn't sell. At the end of the day, the name Johnnie Walker just doesn't mean anything in men's apparel. Consumers couldn't make the leap.

The company would have been much better off, in my opinion, extending their brand based on *flavor profile*. Their scotch has such a unique taste, and that's an easier extension for customers to understand. As with the Baileys coffee creamer, it would have likely been smarter to go a more direct route in leveraging the flavor of the beverage—the pure equity of the brand—rather than developing a lifestyle product. But honestly, you never know.

The jump from alcohol to menswear may seem foolish in retrospect, but in licensing it's surprisingly easy to fall into that trap. Sometimes it's just a matter of office politics and the particular personnel involved. Maybe a brand manager blocks the strategic play that's the right one and makes a leap for something that doesn't work. Then, next thing you know, there's a reorganization at the company and they're trying something completely different.

Interestingly, Johnnie Walker has now ventured into food and is producing branded chocolates.

What is the "pure equity" of your brand?

EQUITY THAT DOESN'T TRANSFER

One of the biggest names in the fast-food space is Burger King. When you think of BK, you think of their signature Whopper, which has been around since 1957. You may also think of onion rings. But you certainly don't think of *apples*.

I'm not talking here about apple slices that come as an optional side with your burger and fries. I'm talking about

Burger King–branded, packaged, pre-sliced apples being sold in supermarkets. Yes, that actually happened.

Source: © Restaurant Brands International

A lot of brands want to play in this space because they want to be seen as healthy. And in the health and nutrition sector, apple slices are indeed a smart bet. Fruit, vegetables, and cut-up salads have all done well in the licensing world. Unfortunately, health and nutrition are also categories where it's very easy to go wrong.

To state the obvious, there was a complete disconnect between the popular hamburger chain, which was fast food, and the licensed product. Of all the brands that you could put on fruit, no one would ever think of Burger King. Imagine a customer at a grocery store: what would make them choose to grab the BK pack of apple slices over Granny Smith or Fuji?

To be sure, Burger King is a brand that has accumulated significant equity. But is there anything about BK that gives equity to *apple slices*? Not at all. The equity simply doesn't transfer. There's no connection between the brand and the product.

On the other hand, if BK were to sell a precooked, flame-grilled frozen burger, I'm sure it'd be a huge success. (BK, if you're reading this, call us and we'll make it happen for you.)

Again, I get why Burger King *wanted* to be in that aisle.

But consumers just didn't see them there. You are what you are, and BK is fast food.

Lots of brands want to be seen as healthy, but not everyone can succeed in that space.

BE TRUE TO YOUR PERSONALITY

To succeed in licensing, you have to understand who you are: not who you *want* to become, but how consumers actually perceive you.

To this end, it's essential that you identify your "brand personality," and in the following chapter we look at a number of licensed products that succeeded precisely because the brand knew who they were in the eyes of their consumers.

Be true to your personality and you'll thrive in brand licensing.

CHAPTER 3

WHAT KIND OF BRAND ARE YOU FUNDAMENTALLY?

Understanding your *brand personality* means getting to the core of what your brand—your reputation—truly means in the minds of consumers. This is where the rubber meets the road in licensing: it's where you succeed or where you fail.

Why is personality so very important? As we saw in the previous chapter with Burger King, you may want to be seen as healthy—or eco-friendly or charitable or luxurious—but if consumers don't think of you that way, your ability to license your brand in any one of those categories is going to be seriously hindered.

When I started out in licensing twenty-two years ago, I represented the estates of many Hollywood legends, including Humphrey Bogart, The Three Stooges, and W.C. Fields. Readers who are a bit longer in the tooth like me will remember that Fields's persona was that of a grumpy old man who hated kids and dogs.

Source: © W.C. Fields Productions Inc.

His grandson, Ron Fields was the point person from the family. Ron was very creative and a great guy. I enjoyed hearing all his stories about his grandfather. One day he let me in on a great secret: "You know, Grandpa didn't actually hate kids. He loved them. That was just a shtick. I think you should really let people know that."

My response: "Let me tell you something, Ron. I am sure you are right, but there's not enough money in the world to convince everybody that W.C. Fields really liked kids," because, let's face it, he was always knocking them.

I wasn't being mean (okay, maybe a little); I was just making a point about brand personalities. No one would ever buy a line of W.C. Fields–branded kids' toys. His persona, his legacy, is just too strong and intense in the opposite direction of the spirit of the product.

I bring this story up because W.C. Fields represents brand personality to the extreme. When you become synonymous with something—as Fields was with misanthropy, hating kids, etc.—the association becomes so ingrained in consumers' minds that it's almost unthinkable to veer in a new direction when you venture into licensing.

Again, brands may *want* to go after a lot of different kinds of products, but that doesn't mean they *should*. When licensing goes wrong, it's usually because the brand doesn't understand how it's perceived among its core customers.

Licensing fails most spectacularly when you don't understand how your brand is perceived.

KNOWING WHO YOU ARE

Having lived in Los Angeles for a long time, I remember going to Wolfgang Puck's first restaurant, Spago, in the eighties. Back then, the Austrian chef would be there himself, working the room. He'd always come over and say hi. It didn't matter if you were Arnold Schwarzenegger or a nobody like me, he treated everybody the same: with genuine graciousness.

You could tell that his warmth came from the heart; it wasn't an act. He really cared about customers and wanted you to feel good when you were in one of his restaurants.

When I think about what Wolfgang Puck represents—his brand personality—it's really about hospitality and trust. Wolfgang *is* the brand, and those traits are what people have always seen in him. As Jeff Bezos says, your personal brand is what people say when you leave the room.

Well, if that's the case, what they say about Wolfgang is

that he's gracious, unpretentious, humble, authentic, the kind of guy you want to hang with. So, when he went out and created a licensing empire with houseware products—including pots, pans, kitchen supplies, cooking utensils, and much more—his personal brand had already laid the foundation for success.

Indeed, for twenty years now, Wolfgang has been selling his products on the Home Shopping Network. He comes across on television the same way he does in person: as if he's inviting you into his own home.

Of course, viewers and consumers are also drawn to what they perceive, rightfully, as world-class food with top-shelf ingredients. Even as Wolfgang himself is approachable, there's an upscale, aspirational quality to his food, like his classic dish of smoked-salmon pizza with caviar. With his licensed products, he retains this passion in the service of bringing quality goods to a broader population at a reasonable price.

Understanding his brand personality has served Wolfgang very well, from his massive constellation of restaurants to his wide array of best-selling products. People feel like they know him, and so they trust what he's selling.

That's what knowing your brand is all about. Yet just as important is knowing who you are *not*. Here, again,

Wolfgang nails it. In fact, we brought his company an opportunity for a line of kitchen furniture, and it was a strong deal financially, with a heavy six-figure guarantee.

Wolfgang declined. He felt that his brand wouldn't bring anything to that space.

In retrospect, he was probably right. Sometimes the best deals are the ones you *don't* do.

If you don't want to tarnish your brand, then at one point or another you'll need to decline a licensing opportunity.

Of course, it's hard for me to say that. As the licensing agency, we would have gotten paid for executing the deal. But I respect Wolfgang immensely for knowing both who he is and who he isn't.

TWO VERY DIFFERENT BRAND PERSONALITIES

If you're unfamiliar with Wolfgang Puck or W.C. Fields, surely you've heard of Apple. It's one of the strongest brands in the world. When you think of Apple, you think of creativity and innovation. In the company's famous "Think Different" ads, they cemented their brand's association with rule-breaking creatives and freethinkers: "Here's to the crazy ones. The misfits. The rebels. The troublemakers. The round pegs in the square holes."

The campaign was brilliant because it made you want to be a person like that. It inspired and allowed you to be better, different, out of the norm—and empowered you to make a difference in the world. Apple understood the first rule of selling: people do not buy products; they buy the better versions of themselves that they aspire to be.

Could their competitor, Microsoft, have made an ad like "Think Different"? Well, they *could* have, but it would have fallen flat. As a brand manifesto, it would have been completely contrary to Microsoft's personality.

When it comes to understanding your brand personality, Apple is the paragon.

Look, obviously Microsoft is a hell of a company too. They were largely responsible for the whole personal computer revolution. But the truth of the matter is that their brand doesn't lend itself these days to creativity in the same way that Apple's does. When it comes to licensing (even if Apple historically hasn't done licensing), Apple's brand gives them a lot more room to play in other categories.

By contrast, Microsoft's brand is buttoned-up. Microsoft PCs were literally portrayed by a suit-and-tie-wearing, stodgy-looking fellow (John Hodgman) in another classic Apple ad campaign called "Get a Mac."

The point is that without a strong understanding of your brand personality—and Apple is the example par excellence here—you are vulnerable and at a disadvantage when it comes to licensing. Especially in today's world, where one negative comment on social media can turn into a nightmare for your brand, clarity and consistency about what you represent is more important than ever.

THE CONCENTRIC CIRCLES OF PRODUCTS

Can you succeed at brand licensing without having the kind of raving fans that Apple does? Of course you can. Not every brand needs to inspire passionate identification. But you still need to have a strong sense of *who you are*.

Let me put it this way: a brand doesn't have to change the world. It can just be good at what it does. Remember Duraflame? As we learned in chapter 2, Duraflame is the leader among fireplaces. When you're a leader in any category, even a niche one like fire logs, you can still mean something important to consumers.

Take, for example, Arm & Hammer. This is a brand that, for much of its history, was known strictly for baking soda. Most people don't even know what to do with baking soda. It's just something that sits in your refrigerator—not what you think of as a sexy product.

And yet, Arm & Hammer has figured out a way to excel in licensing, with almost sixty licensed products in everything from baby care and personal care to pet care, from kitty litter and toothpaste to air filters. How did they do it? How did they take a static product that you basically ignore—something that stays at the back of your fridge for years without replacement—and build that brand into a vast licensing empire?

Your brand doesn't have to change the world to mean the world to consumers.

It wasn't until the 1970s that Arm & Hammer started to think of their product not only as baking soda, but as a broader cleanser that could be used for washing, vacuuming, and more. They looked into what their brand was really all about at its core and found that the common denominator was *deodorizing*.

As a business strategy, deodorizing worked wonders. Even though you're supposed to replace the baking soda in your refrigerator every few months, let's be honest: most of us don't. By contrast, with "consumable" products, you have to continually buy new ones.

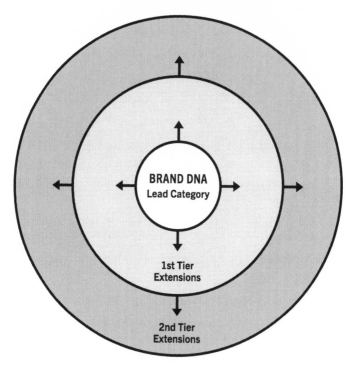

Source: © Global Icons LLC

In my own work as a licensing agent, I use a framework called "concentric circles." In the middle of this model is the "lead category." It represents the DNA of your brand, how consumers really see you. This category acts as the anchor—and once you anchor the category, you can build around it, in a series of concentric circles. You do this by looking at what's closest to the brand, or which categories make the most sense to extend into.

The problem is, brands often want to exceed what makes sense or extend too fast. They attempt this because there's a gap between how they see themselves and how they are seen by consumers. In short, they don't have a strong grasp of their brand personality.

Arm & Hammer may not have been thinking in terms of concentric circles per se, but their logic for extending their brand was likely very similar. They knew that they were seen and trusted when it came to deodorizing ingredients. So, with their core product at the center—and leveraging deodorizing as the key brand promise—they identified categories in proximity to the anchor category: laundry detergent, underarm deodorant, and more.

These are all household items that we live with every day. In fact, every morning when I wake up and every night before I go to bed, I turn to Arm & Hammer toothpaste, which whitens my teeth using a marvelous little thing called...baking soda.

Similarly, one of the biggest categories for the company these days is kitty litter. Kitty litter is all about smell absorption. Arm & Hammer saw the potential in the space, added their special sauce—and now feline deodorizer has become a huge license for the company and one of their most successful products.

Look at how your brand impacts people's lives in a positive way, then build on that.

Through it all, the Arm & Hammer brand has stayed true to the core value of their anchor product. Baking soda is one of the most versatile substances and can be used in a staggering number of ways, from treating insect bites to soothing indigestion and remedying certain diseases. What Arm & Hammer did was simply build on these benefits, in areas where they could make a difference in people's daily lives.

Much has changed for the company in the past 175 years, but much has stayed the same, including their iconic logo of a muscular arm wielding a big hammer. Their longevity is a testament to how they were able to look at their brand honestly and capture the underlying personality.

In fact, Arm & Hammer recently got into another smart category for them: creating a branded diaper pail, which of course is a product built to mask or hide unpleasant odors.

And it just keeps going. Yet another successful extension for Arm & Hammer has been in footcare. They started out making foot powder. And once they saw success, they went even further in the podiatric space, beyond deodorizing, into products like insoles and pads.

In other words: an initial entry into a new category allows you to establish a *foothold*.

ESTABLISHING A FOOTHOLD

One interesting facet of the concentric circle model is the way that you can create little internal circles within a circle. Once consumers trust you in a particular category, it frees you to start doing products that wouldn't necessarily have been brand-appropriate earlier.

When we were working with Ford, our process followed this path. We started with hand tools, then launched into power tools, then generators, and finally power washers. Once consumers trusted the basic hand tools, then motorized power tools made sense to them. Adding electrification to these products, in turn, opened up the door to additional areas.

Ford's trajectory is ideal. Your licensed products may not establish a foothold in the same way. There are all sorts of factors that determine how far you can extend something in any direction. What matters is that you're not resting on your laurels, but rather constantly thinking about ways to broaden your reach.

Consider what would have happened to Arm & Hammer if they had never branched out from baking soda. Would they have lasted? If they hadn't already been established in all those other categories, would their modern-day competitor, Febreze (which uses a chemical to absorb odors, not just mask them), have eaten their proverbial lunch? Would a box of Febreze now be seen in the back of your refrigerator?

We will never know, but what we do know is that savvy brand extension, rooted in an understanding of brand personality, is a peerless way to diversify and protect yourself from disruptive newcomers.

And yet, as we'll see in the next chapter, effective brand licensing is built on not only your brand personality (which helps you figure out *what* to build), but also the particular traits of your customers (which tell you exactly *who* you should be going after). Only then can you create products that leverage who you are and who you are trying to reach.

Brand extension is a peerless way to diversify and protect yourself from disruptive newcomers.

CHAPTER 4

THE DISTINGUISHING TRAITS OF YOUR CUSTOMERS

Caterpillar is primarily known as a manufacturer of industrial machinery and construction equipment. But it is also a work-wear brand that licenses boots built for work sites.

I spoke to the head of Caterpillar licensing, Kenny Beaupre, to ask him about the distinguishing traits of his customers and his approach to brand extensions. He told me that one thing connects all Caterpillar consumers: they want to succeed in their job.

At first, I was confused. Doesn't everyone want to succeed? But Kenny meant something slightly different. He wasn't talking about success in a financial or career sense. Caterpillar products help make customers' jobs *easier* and facilitate their ability to deliver results.

Caterpillar talks about being "champions for success." They make products that give their customers the tools to flourish in whatever their job may be, whether it's paving a road in India or servicing a power generator at a hospital. This is a clear case of what I emphasized earlier: selling is all about helping consumers become their better selves.

Because Caterpillar pursued licensing with this overriding value in mind, there are now 150 Caterpillar-branded merchandise stores around the world. You can buy everything from denim jeans to toolboxes to miniature toys of Caterpillar excavators.

But what intrigued me most was the company's extension into the smartphone market. Caterpillar created a phone that was pretty much indestructible.

Source: © Caterpillar Inc.

Remember: the quintessential Caterpillar consumer is someone who works in construction. As with Ford, a Caterpillar customer needs a product that's hardy, rugged, and durable—something that just works.

When the company thought about the possibility a Caterpillar-branded phone, they looked at the traits of these individuals and asked themselves, "What kind of a phone would someone on a construction site need to succeed?"

After identifying these traits—and then pairing them with the distinguishing traits of their customers—Caterpillar was able to create a terrific licensed product.

WHAT DOES A FORD MUSTANG HAVE IN COMMON WITH NAIL POLISH?

In the opening chapter, I told the story of our "man-cave strategy" license for Ford. But it turns out that Mustang, the popular sports car, has a pretty high *female* demographic. The brand team at Mustang came to us to help them use licensing to better speak to women.

Our team researched the traits and behaviors of these particular consumers. What were their regular routines? What we found was a high-index crossover between female Mustang lovers and the experience of getting a weekly manicure and pedicure. Stereotypical? Perhaps. But that's what the data showed.

In searching for opportunities that made sense and were female-focused, we hit upon the idea of a partnership with OPI, a salon brand, to do nail polishes in the colors of Mustang vehicles. The Mustang drivers were already visiting the salons for their mani-pedis, so the license was perfect for meeting the customer where she was and creating new brand impressions on a recurring basis. (No one buys a car every week, but many people get a weekly beauty treatment.)

Even better, the new nail polishes tied into the colors of the new Mustangs being rolled out at that time for the vehicle's fiftieth birthday. These were cool colors, really different. The connection with the product was especially strong. In theory, you could buy the new car and wear the nail polish that matched it.

What made the whole thing work was, in large part, the extraordinary marketing that OPI did. They promoted the product not only in the salons, but also in print and even on the Jumbotron in Times Square. They ran a fifteen-second spot of the nail lacquer on that Jumbotron every day for a month. It created 500 million brand impressions. Do you know what you'd have to pay to buy something like that?

Don't just go for the first ideas—really stretch to find ones that make the consumer feel good.

Long story short: the licensed products did better than anyone expected, and this was largely thanks to the magnificent efforts of OPI and their executive vice president at the time, Suzi Fischmann. Ford was happy, OPI was happy, and even apart from the money, the promotion did a lot for the Mustang brand. (In chapter 7, we'll cover the importance of choosing the right partner.)

But the bigger takeaway from this story is about looking

at the customer, their traits, and their routines—then figuring out the brand impression that will unleash the highest impact. Clearly, the female Mustang fan had been underserved by Ford's standard marketing. So the company wanted to tap into this subsegment and create buzz around it. Invisible marketing helped them do just that.

SOMETIMES YOUR CUSTOMERS WILL SURPRISE YOU

In looking at the characteristics of your customers, sometimes the real defining trait is *not* the thing that's right under your nose. For example, through market research we learned that consumers for one of our first clients, Igloo, which makes coolers, were bound together not by beer drinking but by a propensity for outdoor activities.

As a result, the first category we licensed for Igloo was gas grills. That might seem like a head-scratcher; a more obvious choice would have been a product whose function is also to keep things cool. But the grills turned out to be a smart target for licensing, because the same customers who grilled in their backyard or on a camping trip always had an Igloo cooler next to them to store their food, condiments, and drinks. The brand, it turned out, was already naturally ingrained in their positive experiences.

Similarly, when the brand Ghost—which makes protein powder and is the market leader in that space—was looking to license, their research showed surprising traits among their health-conscious consumers. These people were exercising a lot, and they would use the protein powder in their daily regimen.

But they were also trying to lose weight and struggling with nighttime cravings. To avoid eating junk food at eleven at night, they would actually eat the protein powder as a semi-healthy alternative.

An outside-the-box idea emerged: if these folks were already eating the powder as an indulgence, why not give it a truly indulgent flavor profile?

As a result of this brainstorm, Ghost reached out to the brand owner of Sour Patch Kids candy with the idea of launching a line of Sour Patch Kids protein powder.

Source: © Ghost Lifestyle

Granted, if you're not a hard-core gym person, you might think this concoction would taste terrible. But Sour Patch Kids protein powder is hugely popular among gym-goers. As soon as it hit the market, the new line exploded.

It turns out that health-conscious customers of these kinds of products *wanted* something super-sweet and candy-like. In fact, the success of the product has now created its own subcategory across the entire protein-powder market.

Sometimes the defining trait of your consumer isn't the thing that's obvious.

CHAPTER 5

MINING FOR GOLD

Here's a bit of Lotman family lore for you: I come from a long line of butchers. My grandfather started his career boning out meat, which my father then sold to supermarkets and one day, to McDonald's.

Source: © Shutterstock

Back then, the meat was shrink-wrapped and put in a tray with a cloth underneath it to keep it from bleeding out. For this reason, they called it "diaper meat" (I know, yuck).

No one uses that unpleasant moniker anymore, but a lot of supermarket meat is still packaged and sold in the same way today: plastic-wrapped in nonbranded plastic with a price-and-weight sticker and lined up in counters across the butcher section.

This is a perfect example of what we refer to as a "white space": a retail category where no one's thought of going before, in a licensing sense. Sure, there are some brands in the meat section these days. The normal players like Perdue and Tyson, for example, are doing marinated meats. But until recently, the meat section remained wide open.

Now, finally, we're seeing things like Budweiser lines of pork, sausage, and beer brats. Not to mention Tony Roma's ribs and Guinness beer-battered fish.

I love the case study of diaper meat, and not just because of my family connection. It's a white space that everyone can understand and relate to (well, maybe not vegetarians), and it reveals how enormous the opportunity is in the world of brand licensing.

Why would people want to buy a branded meat product instead of a generic one? It's not just about the stamp of approval; it's also about the added value. Generally, people don't like to spend a ton of time cooking. Products like Tony Roma's ribs make life easier. Simple as that.

This is why white spaces are such a win-win. The new product commands a higher profit margin, while not competing on the commodity market. Consumers are willing to pay a premium for a name they value and trust. Meanwhile, the brand itself gets to grow and expand.

What white spaces can you think of?

Continuing with supermarkets, what about fish? No one has really branded the fish and seafood area. Walk into your local Pathmark or Kroger and you'll find generic plastic-wrapped shrimp and swordfish.

Why haven't more brands come into these spaces? Who's going to be first? Licensing in white spaces is like mining for gold. It's a land grab. You want to be the pioneer.

UNCOVERING HIDDEN PLACES

Consider the travel category. Sure, there are individual travel agents out there, and some brands like Abercrombie & Kent have been around for a while. But what about companies that arrange international tours and study-abroad programs for young people?

I became interested in this space on a personal level when my eldest daughter, Anna Sophia, who was fifteen at the time, did a two-week summer program in Fiji that was licensed by National Geographic.

Remarkably, the program had already been running for ten years. It was a partnership between Nat Geo and a company called Putney. The concept was that students would choose a topic and then visit a country that was relevant to that area of learning for study.

Clearly, these tours were licensed; they weren't actually run by Nat Geo. But I have to admit, even though I'm an insider to this licensing game, as a parent it made a notable difference to my peace of mind that the program came with an imprimatur I knew and trusted.

Your average customer certainly never knew that another company, Putney, ran the tours. The whole thing was fully branded with Nat Geo's name and logo.

I'm happy to report that Anna Sophia had a great time on the trip. As for me, I gained even more respect for National Geographic for being such a white-space pioneer: for seeing the opportunity to bring their well-known brand into a virgin category. In fact, the *New York Times* recently launched a similar program (by the way, she took that one too).

Get out of the office and go look at all forms of retail.

LUXURY BRANDING IN WHITE SPACES

Historically, real estate has been a white space as well. But one developer in Miami recently bucked that trend. Dezer Development was building a high-rise luxury apartment building. While the property was very exclusive and came with lots of amenities, it needed a point of differentiation. Dezer thought to themselves, "Why not attach a brand and a corresponding aesthetic?"

They ended up approaching Armani to design all the interiors. The idea was that the partnership would transfer to Dezer's real estate project the same luxury halo carried by Armani products.

Ultimately, they launched what's now called the Armani Casa in Miami. These are luxury condos that are consistent in every way with Armani's exclusive brand. Because Armani is a designer, it was a given that he—Giorgio Armani himself—would be actively involved.

Dezer's entry into the white space of real estate with

Armani was a smashing success, and they soon repeated it with a Porsche-branded luxury high-rise. Other developers followed suit: there are the Lamborghini condos in Dubai, and a company named Cerbera owns the rights to a Fendi Chateau in Florida. Also in Miami, there's an Aston Martin real estate project where the condos sell for up to $50 million.

As you can see, one thing leads to another. But it all starts with identifying a white space and using the intellectual property from a third party—and the whole aura that goes with it—to lure the consumer.

THE "DUH" MOMENT

Sometimes it just boggles the mind that no one has thought to use licensing to add excitement to a boring category. Take whipped cream. It's a product that's been around *forever*. When I was a kid, you had your dairy whipped and nondairy whipped, your light and full fat. In fact, for seventy years, there were just two types: frozen or in an aerosol can.

Finally, in recent years, Hershey launched a Hershey's flavored whipped cream and a Reese's flavored whipped cream. Now, all of a sudden, there's a mad rush to add flavoring, as a point of differentiation, to what was basically a one-flavor category for its entire existence.

Source: © The Hershey Company

How is it that people have walked by the whipped cream shelf their whole life and no one's asked, "Why don't we add some flavor to that? Maybe the consumer will buy more"?

It seems so simple.

It's the same thing with kosher grape juice. For years, there was Manischewitz and that was that—until Welch's got in the game. The opportunity couldn't have been more obvious. Welch's is one of the biggest brands in grape jams and juices. They could stretch into this new space and instantly grab a pretty good market share, just by virtue of name recognition.

And that's exactly what they did. They partnered with Manischewitz to bring to the kosher section a 100 percent grape juice. Now it's everywhere.

> Sometimes the opportunity to move into a white space is a no-brainer.

TIMING IS EVERYTHING

As much as I joke about people missing the boat with this or that opportunity, sometimes the reality is that the market just isn't ready for the particular branded product.

For example, baby stroller companies have been involved in licensing for a long time, but it wasn't until recently that someone thought of—or rather, someone decided to put into action the idea of—marketing a stroller specifically branded to *fathers*. That someone was Maclaren, which partnered with BMW for a stroller targeted toward dads.

In this case, the white space wasn't the category; the white space was the new customer.

Notably, this was a white space that nobody could have penetrated twenty years earlier. Back then, fathers weren't marketed to as consumers of parenting products.

You see, timing is everything; you have to do things in a

certain order. In the case of Maclaren, by the time they put out their male-oriented BMW stroller, they had already seen success targeting moms with Burberry strollers and other similar products. And let's face it: Maclaren makes a hell of a product and has done so for over fifty years.

The BMW stroller was a beaut. It was leather and had the same styling as the interior of a luxury Beemer, down to the stitching and wheels. It was designed *like a BMW*, which imbued the stroller with a masculine "ultimate driving machine" feel.

Source: © Bayerische Motoren Werke AG & Maclaren

Sometimes the white space isn't a category. It's a customer.

As we've seen throughout this chapter, there's great value to be unlocked in white spaces. Moreover, once you create your own product inside a white space, you can often build on that success with another product that's close to the first one.

CHAPTER 6

TARGETING COMPATIBLE PRODUCTS

When marketers talk about "stickiness," what we mean is getting customers to stay with your brand. In order to get them to stick around, we have to develop ways to *keep* them stuck. And nothing is stickier than jelly.

Take Welch's, which has been in the jelly business forever. In chapter 5, we learned how this brand took over the white space of kosher grape juice. This is a perfect example of "crossing the aisle," something that every brand wants, because it expands their reach—and allows consumers to then find the brand's name in a new and unexpected area of the store. With Welch's, instead of being stuck in the "jam" or "condiment" section, or even the "juice" section, now they were in the "kosher" section.

Yet Welch's biggest license to date is not grape juice. It's fruit snacks.

Source: © Welch Foods Inc.

These gummies were one of the first food items that the brand licensed, and the product has since grown into its own $100-million business. It's now a staple in any fruit-snack aisle (as well as the Lotman family pantry).

From the beginning, Welch's fruit snacks dominated their space. Not only that, but the licensee they work with—Promotion in Motion—has also delivered the product to a variety of nontraditional spaces like airports, movie theaters, and vending machines. These extensions allow Welch's to reach the customer outside the grocery store.

In this way, Welch's not only crossed the aisle, but also crossed distribution channels. Whenever I travel, I see the gummies. They're in all the airport stores—bags and bags of the stuff. Airports, of course, are a venue that Welch's would never have infiltrated if they were still only selling grape jelly.

Everyone wants their brand to be found in surprising places that consumers don't necessarily expect. Create your new connection the right way, and your customer becomes that more willing and more likely to stick with you.

How can you cross the aisle and a distribution channel?

Welch's fruit snacks are an excellent example of targeting a product that's adjacent to, but highly compatible with, the original brand. Welch's knew they'd be able to deliver the actual fruit juice to make the snacks. That alone was a strong starting point.

But beyond that, licensing provided the opportunity to get core product into the hands of many more people for a totally different eating occasion. With grape jelly, you have to spread it onto something with a knife. With fruit snacks, you just pop 'em into your mouth, anytime, anywhere.

It didn't hurt, either, that the fruit-snack category has traditionally been perceived as a healthy one. Whether that label is accurate is up for debate. But it probably appealed to Welch's that they'd be able to create a product that didn't deviate from the healthy brand of their core juice product.

Similarly, while no one would mistake Coca-Cola for a healthy product, in 2019 the beverage maker crossed the aisle with a collaboration with Tic Tac. Obviously, Coca-Cola is sold in the soda aisle. But now, with this brand extension, they're in the impulse-buy area, right by the cashier, where consumers are waiting in line and may grab a little something extra at the last minute to toss into their cart.

Forget about the money Coke will make from this partnership. Coca-Cola flavored Tic Tacs are a sensational example of crossing the aisle.

CROSSING AISLES TO OVERCOME BRAND CHALLENGES

Crock-Pot is the number one slow cooker in the country. But they had a couple of challenges as a brand. One was the name "Crock-Pot": it had become so ubiquitous that it was now synonymous with "slow cooker" in the same way that "Kleenex" is synonymous with "facial tissues."

While that may sound like a good thing, it also means that Crock-Pot may one day lose control of their own name. Because people think "Crock-Pot" is the name of the product itself, what happens, ironically, is that the brand identity gets diluted, or even erased.

The other challenge, Crock-Pot's consumer research showed, was that there's a barrier to using a slow cooker: it can take up to eight hours to cook a meal in a Crock-Pot, and you have to do all the preparation yourself. As a result of all this time and work, although people were buying the product—it's one of the most popular gifts on bridal registries—many weren't actually using it.

So Crock-Pot came to us and asked if licensing could help. Yes, it could!

First, we licensed seasonings (to flavor the products in the Crock-Pots), then we licensed meal kits to place in the Crock-Pots. These collaborations meant that consumers no longer had to use their own seasonings, thus greatly reducing the dreaded prep time.

With these licenses, Crock-Pot crossed the aisle. The slow cooker had always been in the "appliance" aisle, but now, thanks to those meal kits, the brand had visibility in the "consumable" aisle as well, alongside the kits and seasonings.

Next, Crock-Pot approached Kroger. The idea was called "Crocktober," and it would take place every October and feature both the slow cooker and licensed product in the middle of these aisles. This added yet another category: "housewares."

All told, consumers found the products together and there were no other slow cookers on display to compete with. Crock-Pot was in the middle of the aisle every "Crocktober," in the fall, when most people use their slow cookers for dishes like chilis and stews.

Cross the aisle with the right product and you can kill two birds with one stone: solving a specific brand challenge and expanding your brand's reach into a new area.

LIKE MAGIC SUPER

In some cases, licensing a compatible product not only

helps solve your particular brand challenges, but can also save your brand from extinction.

For example, Magic Chef is an appliance brand that's sold these days only in Home Depot. Most people, at least those under fifty, don't know them, but they've been around for over eighty-five years. They hired us to make their brand more relevant again.

At Home Depot, you can find Magic Chef in microwave ovens, compact refrigerators, and ice makers. But with our licensing program, Magic Chef is now in a ton of other categories: kitchen gadgets, cookware, air fryers, water coolers, and appliance cleaners. What's more, these products are also going into new retail channels (places like T.J. Maxx, HomeGoods, and dollar stores), all of which place the brand in the hands of new consumers.

Magic Chef's core products, their appliances, are still only sold in Home Depot. The reason for that is not especially interesting: Magic Chef was at one time owned by Whirlpool, until one of their licensees, a Korean company that was doing compact kitchen electrics, ended up buying the brand outright. Because of a noncompete agreement with Whirlpool, we can't put Magic Chef back into big appliances until 2021.

Ultimately, we hope to get the appliances into other channels. When we do, both the consumer and buyer will have already had a good deal of interaction with the brand.

That's because awareness of the brand has been heightened by their licensed products and all the different places they're sold. Their brand has become stickier. And when the time comes, these extensions will help Magic Chef compete with the big boys of appliances.

Availability and visibility are key to raising brand awareness.

What we're doing with Magic Chef is essentially relaunching the brand. Which means we have to give it as much reach as possible.

This is a long play, but by laying the groundwork and getting these licensed products into so many places—particularly less-footprint-intensive categories where they're clip-stripped in and don't take up much space (think, for example, of a ladle or oven mitt)—we slowly but surely make the name "Magic Chef" better known and more trusted.

In the end, the hope is that by crossing aisles and distribution channels with these smaller products, by building awareness through availability and visibility, we'll succeed in bringing the original brand back to life.

COMPATIBLE PRODUCTS ARE AN ANTIDOTE TO SHRINKING SPACES

In some cases, however, it's not only the brand that has fallen out of fashion, but the very nature of the core product. Take, for example, car wax.

When it comes to cleaning and protecting your automobile, there aren't many people out there who still DIY it. That's a problem for a brand like Turtle Wax that's been around for more than half a century.

To help them uncover new customers, we've licensed brushes and polishers that you can use the wax with; hand vacuums for cleaning your car in general; and air fresheners that make your car smell good.

Yet even with these efforts, it's an uphill battle. The consumer base for Turtle Wax is heavily male; female waxers are elusive. And the section of the store that Turtle Wax is usually found in is tiny.

So, having these other product categories allows Turtle Wax to gain more face time with more consumers. It's often the little things that make a brand sticky, especially when they provide recurring interactions.

Source: © Turtle Wax

Finally, some of the licensed products we did with Turtle Wax allowed them to cross distribution channels, just as Welch's did with their fruit snacks. For example, we did a pet protectant seat cover that's now sold in the pet aisle at Target, a place where you otherwise would never find Turtle Wax.

Same thing with car washes: normally these wouldn't be a home for the brand, because the car wash is doing the polishing itself. Why would they need Turtle Wax? Simple: because some of the above licensed products are sold there.

Use licensing to create recurring interactions with your consumers.

It's worth mentioning that even if a market is not shrinking per se, targeting compatible products can serve as an antidote to other specific business limitations. For example, we talked earlier about Duraflame. We worked with them to license indoor heaters and fireplaces, which helped the company tremendously because they allowed Duraflame to spread out their sales across the calendar year.

Indeed, traditionally Duraflame's business has depended on fourth-quarter sales. And the company only made fire logs, which meant Duraflame's name appeared only in one area of a store. Licensing allowed them to appear in a different department and transcend seasonality.

For example, if the winter is light, log sales will plunge.

So the fact that Duraflame can now offset that loss with sales of space heaters, patio heaters, and fireplaces has been a dream come true.

The partnership with Duraflame was a happy one all around. For one, heaters were a category that made a lot of sense: indoor heat stands at the core of Duraflame's brand. And now, the product is an actual heater instead of a log.

What's more, for the Duraflame deal, we had a great partner: a private-label firm that was also the manufacturer for Kirkland. The opportunity to own a brand was very intriguing to them. Another firm could have offered a better deal, but we knew nobody would be a better fit.

In the next chapter, we'll look at why it's so important to have not only the right product, but also the right *partner*.

CHAPTER 7

THE RIGHT PARTNER

As we saw in chapter 4 with Mustang, to do licensing right, you have to find the right partner. Without a passionate and involved licensee like OPI, those branded nail polishes wouldn't have worked nearly as well. OPI was an active partner through and through: they came to Dearborn and, crucially, went above and beyond with their promotion (remember the Times Square Jumbotron?). Such immersion made all the difference.

Same with Maclaren. BMW could easily have worked with any number of stroller companies. But above all, they wanted a partner that wouldn't just check a box but integrate the DNA from BMW's cars into the stroller.

Maclaren was perfect. Not only did they deliver a beautiful new interior fabric, but they also used special materials and made sure the wheels were tooled from scratch. Because they shared BMW's vision and passion, they were able to take an ordinary stroller to another level. In short, they *invested* in the product (the M series).

Ultimately, when dads went to buy the BMW stroller, the product delivered the same luxurious cachet you'd expect from a BMW car.

Other stroller companies had been hungry to win the license, but only Maclaren was willing to put their resources into new hardware and engineering rather than simply repurposing elements they'd used before. As a result, the BMW stroller is a true work of art, from the finely crafted leather to the plush handle design.

Find a partner that respects the unique equities of your brand.

Maclaren is a company that does a lot of products, and usually these are one season in and one season out. That's what the brand is known for: limited, seasonal products. They make a handful of these exclusive goods, sell them out, and do it again next season with a different item.

But the BMW stroller was so successful that they kept doing it.

It goes to show that when you have the right partner that's willing to invest in your brand, you can get an extraordinary product that connects with consumers in a way that lasts.

Yet in order for that connection to happen, you have to do your due diligence. You have to really look into what level of commitment, financial and otherwise, a licensee can and will make to your brand.

Then, based on that info, you have to gauge how well their investment matches your objectives. A lot of potential licensees want to close a deal in the hope that they can then build their business off your brand. Don't let yourself be fooled by companies like that.

Maclaren invested up front in the stroller because the company believed this commitment would pay off in the end—and it did. But not every manufacturer will have such long-term vision and the consummate resources.

As for BMW, they were—and are—exceedingly happy with the collaboration. And a big reason is that in Maclaren they found the perfect partner. Indeed, Maclaren's commitment to the project has proved much more valuable than many other factors that brands tend to obsess over.

THE VALUE OF STRATEGIC THINKING

There was a time and place—especially when licensing

was experiencing a renaissance by way of the entertainment industry—when it seemed like all that a brand cared about was the financial terms of a deal (namely, large advances and high minimum guaranteed payments).

That was all fine and well when there were lots of retailers and the opportunity cost of going with one company over another was significant. But eventually the more sophisticated A-level manufacturers became less willing to pony up large guarantees. Meanwhile, many emerging companies would throw money at brands to win these licenses, and so the licensors became punch-drunk with terms that were extravagant.

The problem is, these arrangements blinded folks to making the smarter play with the right company that maybe wasn't willing to guarantee as much but had more potential overall. The licensors were looking only at the numbers and going with the biggest deal. That kind of myopia generally had an adverse effect in the grand scheme of things.

It's not just about cash. It's about growing your brand.

I can't stress this enough: short-term revenue is *not* what's most important. Even on a financial level, advances and guarantees are less important than royalties.

As we've seen again and again, invisible marketing is

incredibly powerful—but it takes time. You can't think about it in terms of quarter-by-quarter results. This isn't about getting rich overnight. As a matter of fact, it takes between eighteen and twenty-four months just to get on a shelf—and two to three *years* before any real money is made.

Licensing is like relationships: find a partner you're going to want to be with for a long time.

You also need to be willing to help them along, to give them as much support as you can to make *them* successful. Yes, they're investing in your brand. But *you* have to invest in your brand too.

In a way, the "licensee is your customer," as Carlos Coroalles, formerly of Jarden Consumer Solutions, used to say. The licensee is out there busting their hump for you, spending their money and time to extend your brand. You need to do everything you can to bolster them—because when they succeed, you succeed.

Remember: a licensing partnership is a two-way street. In the case of the strollers, it wasn't only Maclaren investing their resources. BMW, too, was very hands-on in bringing Maclaren into their design studio, letting them see the leather and other design elements early on, and generally bringing them behind the curtain. There was a mutual trust and engagement that's essential to any fruitful licensing relationship.

THE WRONG PARTNER

What are the consequences of choosing the wrong partner?

Let's say you do a watch deal with a car brand and the watch doesn't work. Afterward, it'll be exceedingly hard to find a new partner, because everyone will remember the flop.

Here's a famous story. Over twenty years ago, when Taco Bell teamed up with Kraft on a number of Taco Bell-branded products, word on the street was that the Kraft goods didn't deliver. The product was substandard, and it failed miserably.

In this case, it wasn't the end of the world. But the companies did have to go back to the proverbial drawing board, reformulate, and relaunch.

To be sure, Taco Bell Kraft products are still very much around today, so the story has a happy ending. Yet that was by no means a foregone conclusion. At the time, the initial misfire did more harm than good for Taco Bell's brand—so much so that they had to pull the products from the shelf.

Source: © Yum Brands

When you rush things and don't deliver the equity your customers expect, you run the very real risk of tarnishing your brand.

Choosing the wrong partner can be the kiss of death.

MORE THAN THE MONEY

As you leverage the power of licensing, always remind yourself that it's not about the money—it's about the brand. If you're looking at licensing purely to boost revenue, you're taking a narrow-minded view of a program that's loaded with possibilities.

Licensing is about connecting to your customers and letting them find you in different areas. It's about marketing. That's the whole name of the game.

What's more, your licensees are doing most of the work for you. They're out there blocking and tackling with retailers to get shelf space, to publicize your product. The least you can do is help them succeed.

If you think it's only about the money, then you're approaching licensing the wrong way.

CHAPTER 8

BRAND COLLABORATIONS

What is a brand *collaboration*, and how is that different from brand *licensing*?

This is a nuance that sometimes gets lost in my industry. When Adidas did limited-edition sneakers made by Prada in Italy, that wasn't a license but a collaboration. That's because the focus was on sharing a moment of rarified air rather than developing a lasting business.

Brand owners—whether they're in fashion, sports, or whatever the case may be—are always looking to connect with their consumers in unexpected ways, and one of the best ways to do that is a limited collaboration with another brand. Often, the quantity of the given product is small and it sells out almost immediately. But the visibility and engagement are so high that it's more than worth it.

Even though these short-term partnerships sometimes generate royalties, their purpose is more about brand impressions. Usually, one brand is lucky to have the other brand give them an audience or an engagement with a consumer they're trying to reach.

In 2018, for example, Budweiser collaborated with a much-hyped fashion brand called Undefeated. It was a short-term project that consisted of seven to ten SKU (stock-keeping unit) pieces.

What happens next is quite special: not only do people buy the items, but they also post images online, and some even sell them on the secondary market using websites like StockX. Overall, the circumstances create a unique, immersive experience for both consumer and brand.

Usually, these collaborations are for one season, but since 2018 we've seen a lot of one-month partnerships that create instant buzz, especially among millennials and Gen Zers.

You could call these "limited licensing deals." But, again, they're often not about the money but rather two brands coming together to do something different. It doesn't have to be a collection: it could be just two or three SKUs, or even a single item. The point is, you're creating a high-profile touchpoint to extend your brand.

> Short-term, limited-edition collaborations create a unique, immersive experience for both consumer and brand.

BRAND COLLABORATIONS IN THE FASHION WORLD

Fred Segal, the legendary Los Angeles clothing store, was an early pioneer in these types of collaborations. In fact, this was a big part of what drew me to them when I became the owner of the retailer in 2019.

Here's a quick history of this brand. It started in 1961 with a guy named, well, Fred Segal, who had a men's shop. He thought it would be cool to take jeans, which were pretty common back then, and tailor them, which was uncommon. He would tighten them at the top and flare them out at the bottom. In so doing, Fred Segal literally invented the fashion jean category.

He'd even give the jeans out at a bar across the street where all the cool people congregated. Everybody who worked there started wearing them. These folks were his own early version of "influencers." People would ask, "Where'd you get those jeans?" and the bartenders or hostesses would say, "Across the street, at Fred Segal."

Believe it or not, that was the birth of the fashion jean industry—and much of Fred Segal's success in the five decades since has been around these collaborations. They specialize in executing these limited-edition partnerships that engender huge buzz and anticipation (what the kids today call "FOMO," or "fear of missing out" on the hottest new trend).

Since I came on board at Fred Segal, we've continued this winning tradition by partnering with brands such as Wrangler and CB2. For the former, Wrangler put up a display in our fourteen-hundred-square-foot pop-up space to showcase their vintage products. We're now using this pilot to launch a Wrangler co-branded Fred Segal line, which will be sold at retail.

Source: © Fred Segal LLC & Wrangler

This collaboration thrills me. Jeans are such a part of our heritage in this country, and Wrangler has been around forever. It's great for *them* because they get to share the rarified air that Fred Segal brings. But it's also great for *us* because Wrangler is an iconic American brand that makes great jeans.

With CB2, the scenario was similar: they came to Fred Segal wanting to do something around the cool LA lifestyle. This, after all, is the space that Fred Segal owns, and so the project was projected to be an in-and-out, one-season-only collaboration.

The project was a big hit—so much so that it's still here three years later. How did this happen? It's a given that the products and design were great. But more importantly, the teams worked into the products the zeitgeist of LA culture: that whole outdoor, hanging-by-the-pool vibe. Because of that, not only did the parties boost awareness, but they also broke into new markets.

This is the beauty of ad hoc brand collaborations. Of course, the distinguishing feature is the managed scarcity of the product. By limiting the supply of the goods, you create a second-market drive, where the product continues to be sold (after it sells out) but at a much higher price. You also, almost always, see that the buzz enjoys a second life on social media. Engagement with the brand lasts longer than it normally would because the product is so special and scarce.

Once you become aware of these collaborations, you'll start seeing them all the time. For example, you've probably heard of Taco Bell's Doritos Locos Tacos. The product took off like crazy. All they did was sprinkle some nacho cheese dust and wrap the taco in a Doritos-esque bag, but it sparked such demand that they've now sold over a billion units.

Similarly, inspired by Jack Daniel's Tennessee Honey whiskey, Jack Daniel's did a Nike collaboration for custom Air Force 1 sneakers. There were only sixty-seven pairs, and they were raffled off during NBA All-Star Weekend at the brand's pop-up store in Los Angeles. It's hard to build that kind of momentum on your own.

Collaborating with another brand is a great way to connect with your customer, boost awareness, and break into new markets.

CHAPTER 9

THE STUFF EVERYONE HATES

Contracts are a necessary evil. No one likes them. In fact, almost everyone hates them. Yet the fact is, you *must* heed them closely. If you go into a contract negotiation without the necessary background knowledge, you'll likely make mistakes that will haunt you for years to come.

Over the past twenty-two years, I've seen it time and again: people get trapped in terrible deals because they don't understand what they're getting into. For example, consider the license between the cookie company Mrs. Fields and Maxfield Chocolates. It's a classic example of what *not* to do. Because Mrs. Fields negotiated the license themselves and didn't know which terms were important in this kind of agreement, they wound up tethered *for perpetuity* to this particular chocolate manufacturer.

What a mess.

At the time they did the deal, it probably all seemed fine. Mrs. Fields was likely happy with a new revenue stream, and they considered the project small potatoes anyway.

Yet because of the onerous terms, Mrs. Fields didn't get anything out of the deal in terms of marketing or extending their brand. All they got were royalties. That's helpful if you need a short-term boost in sales, but brands that endure focus on the big picture and the long term.

Sadly, there's nothing Mrs. Fields can do at this point. "Perpetuity" means *forever*. And it could have all been avoided. But the franchise cookie company was unfamiliar with licensing and didn't even realize that a deal like this *could* go on forever.

That's just one example. Here's another thing to be on the lookout for: don't give up global territory rights or multiple product categories with no claw back provisions. If the licensee doesn't deliver, you need the ability to start anew with someone else.

Make sure you retain claw back rights.

Finally, let me share another contractual lesson. All too often, corporate lawyers will tell their clients, "Oh, I can do a license agreement—after all, I've written contracts before."

The truth is, many lawyers don't understand the fundamentals of these deals. After all, licensing is a very specific type of legal contract, and the last thing you want is to hire a generalist for work that's specialized.

Indeed, to participate in brand licensing and not know the ins and outs of your contracts is nuts. Unfortunately, it's also very common. Which is why, in the next few pages, you'll read more about business plans, deal memos, and product approvals.

Is this stuff boring? Yes. But it's also essential.

THE BUSINESS PLAN

Whenever you meet a licensee, you should insist they provide a business plan. They need to demonstrate who they are, how big they are, how long they've been in business, and, ideally, what other licenses they have.

Furthermore, the plan should outline where they sell, their banking references, what they expect to do with your brand or brands, and, of course, their licensing experience.

If someone isn't willing to invest the time to provide these details, that's a big red flag. If they can't clear that initial hurdle, how can you expect them to invest their resources in something that could be years in the making?

Along the same lines, you don't just want to haphazardly make a deal with the first person who calls you and says they love your brand. The first person who comes through the door isn't likely to be the one you want to be in business with. Sometimes it is, but most of the time it isn't.

Instead, you usually need to interview three to four companies. If you're hiring an agency to help you, you'll have a leg up because, hopefully, they already know most of the players in your area and have dealt with them before.

If someone isn't willing to develop a business plan, they're likely not your ideal partner.

Global Icons

Trademark License Application

If applicable, attach a Company Overview and Capabilities Deck

Company Information

Company Legal Name:		Website Address:	
Legal Form of Company:	State of Jurisdiction:	Public or Private:	
Current address:			
City:	State:	ZIP Code:	
Yrs in Business:	2018 Gross* Sales: $_____	2017 Gross Sales: $_____	2016 Gross Sales: _____
Parent Company (if any):	Current Address:		
City:	State:	ZIP Code:	

Describe your company and background (you may provide a separate presentation that shows your company's capabilities and background):

What owned and licensed brands along with products do you currently market and what % is attributable to your overall sales:

Have you had any product recalls within last 7 years? If so, please list and include how you resolved it:

List all judgments, suits, liens, bankruptcies, UCC filings:

Ownership and Management Information

If company is not a corporation, provide a list of all Principal Owners (name, title, address):

List shareholders and number of shares (if any):

Primary Contact (include name and title):	E-mail:	Phone:
Secondary Contact (include name and title):	E-mail:	Phone:
President:	E-mail:	Phone:
Sales Contact:	E-mail:	Phone:
PD/Art Contact:	E-mail:	Phone:
Finance Contact:	E-mail:	Phone:

If you are private and cannot disclose Gross Sales Dollars, please include a range, such as:
Under $500K, $500K-$1MM, $1-2MM, $2-5MM, $5-10MM, $10-20MM, $20-30MM, $30-50MM, $50MM-100MM,
$100MM-300MM, $300-600MM, $600MM-900MM, $900MM-1B, Over $1B

Financial Information

Bank Reference and Contact Name:		
Current address:		
City:	State:	ZIP Code:
Phone:	E-mail:	Fax:
D&B # (if applicable):	Most recent D&B rating:	

Sales and Distribution Information

1

Source: © Global Icons LLC

Global Icons

If you are doing business internationally, in what countries/regions do you currently have retail distribution and what % of business is done in each one:

Describe your sales capability (direct sales, reps, agents, distributors/brokers, etc.):

How many retail doors carry your products in the United States:

Who are your top 5 retailers:

List your Retail Distribution Channels and the % of sales volume (e.g., Mass Market = Walmart, Target; Drug = CVS; Clubs = Costco; Mid-Tier = JCP, Kohl's; Upstairs Dept = Nordstrom, Macy's; Off-Price = TJ Maxx; Office = Staples; Dollar = Dollar General; Other Specialty = Auto, Home, and others that are special to this category)

Channel	% Sales	Requested Channel	Key Accounts
Mass Market	____%	Y/N	List Key Accounts
Drug	____%	Y/N.	List Key Accounts
Warehouse Clubs	____%	Y/N	List Key Accounts
Souvenir/Duty Free	____%	Y/N	List Key Accounts
Bookstores	____%	Y/N	List Key Accounts
Toy Stores	____%	Y/N	List Key Accounts
Grocery Stores	____%	Y/N	List Key Accounts
Mid-Tier Department Stores	____%	Y/N	List Key Accounts
Upstairs Department Stores	____%	Y/N	List Key Accounts
Specialty Stores	____%	Y/N	List Key Accounts
Convenience Stores	____%	Y/N	List Key Accounts
Home Improvement/Hardware	____%	Y/N	List Key Accounts
Office Products	____%	Y/N	List Key Accounts
Art & Craft (Michael's)	____%	Y/N	List Key Accounts
Off-Price Retail	____%	Y/N	List Key Accounts
E-commerce/Catalog	____%	Y/N	List Key Accounts
Other Specialty List	____%	Y/N	List Key Accounts

Manufacturing Information

Do you own and/or operate all your manufacturing facilities:

Do you and your third-party manufacturers (if any) comply with all applicable laws (Global Icons and our clients will not do business with companies that violate the law and will terminate licensees):

Please list below all manufacturing facilities, including: (1) company name; (2) location; (3) contact name; (4) e-mail and phone; (5) ISO compliant?; (6) how often are they audited:

Have any of your manufacturing facilities been certified by a major national retailer? If so, which retailers:

Do you have a code of conduct:	Describe how you ensure all manufacturers comply with your code of conduct and/or standards:

Describe criteria used for your quality control program:

Describe your selection process of third-party manufacturers:

References (retailers and licensors)

Company & Contact:	E-mail:	Phone:

Proposal

Proposed Brand/Property:	

2

Source: © Global Icons LLC

Proposed Category:	Detailed Product Description:
Proposed Category:	Detailed Product Description:
Proposed Category:	Detailed Product Description:

If you currently sell a product similar to the proposed products, what was the wholesale dollar volume for the most recent year (include fiscal year dates):		
Projected retail presentation dates:	Projected ship date:	Projected on-shelf date:
Any retailer resets that would affect sell-in for the proposed products:		What tradeshows will you showcase the proposed licensed products:
Proposed Territory:	Proposed Royalty Rate:	List targeted accounts for each distribution channel:
Do you plan on digital marketing, advertising, PR, etc:	Launch Year marketing spend: $	Ongoing % of sales that will be spent on marketing:

What is your vision for the licensed program—product positioning and how will it fit into your overall portfolio:

How will the proposed licensed product be differentiated in the competitive set (innovations, positioning, etc.):

What is the size of the market for the proposed licensed category along with the top market leaders:

Projected Wholesale Sales

Product	Wholesale Price	Year 1 (18 months)	Year 2	Year 3	Year 4
		Provide Sales Range – Conservative / Medium / Stretch Goal			

Please provide your assumptions that you used to project these sales (such as x/y/z retailer in # of doors, etc.):

Supplemental Items

Please provide additional details about your go-to-market strategy along with goals for the proposed licensed products:

If applicable, please forward the following documents:
- annual report/financial statement
- manufacturer audit report(s)
- ISO certificates
- quality/efficacy testing of proposed product

Prospective Licensee Statement

The information in this application is true and correct to the best of my knowledge. I understand that this is an application only and does not constitute an agreement. I agree not to utilize any of the proposed trademarks/logos without a fully executed license agreement. I acknowledge that Global Icon's client may license other products similar to mine without obligations to me.

Signature of Applicant:	Date:
Print Name:	Title:

Thank you for your interest in our client's brand(s). Your application will be carefully reviewed and considered. Please allow ample time to review and provide feedback. If it meets the client's initial criteria, we will provide you with a Deal Term Letter that outlines terms for your review and approval. If we both agree to the Letter, we will submit a Deal Memo for our client's review and approval. If they approve the Deal Memo, we will then work on the long-form License Agreement.

3

Source: © Global Icons LLC

THE DEAL MEMO

After you get the business plan and see that it's sound, the next step is to start putting together potential terms. You use this framework to develop a "deal sheet" or "deal term letter," a nonbinding agreement that helps all parties reach an understanding before you get to the contract stage.

DEAL MEMO

Salesperson:
Agreement Type: Merchandise License   Permission License
Memo/Agreement Date:
Licensor:
Licensee:
Licensed Properties:
Product:
Term: FROM _____ TO _____
Territory:
Advance/Fee:
Guarantee (Including Advance):
Distribution:
Latest In-Store Date:
Number of Samples:
Third-Party Manufacturer (Yes or No):
End of Sell-Off:
Other (including renewal options):

Financials:				
ID	Description	Amount	Due Date	Type Description

Royalties:				
ID	Clause	Type	Rate	Applies To

Approved by Client: _____ Date: _____

Approved by Supervisor: _____ Date: _____

Source: © Global Icons LLC

DEAL TERM LETTER

DATE:

CONTACT:

ADDRESS:

Dear CONTACT:

This sets down in writing, as a convenience to facilitate further discussions, some of the proposed deal terms for a potential license agreement between LICENSOR and LICENSEE. This represents simply the state of our discussions to date. No agreements have been reached or decisions made on the basis of this summary, nor should any be implied based on the existence of this summary.

Licensed Material:
Category:
Articles:
Exclusivity: Nonexclusive
Term: X yrs (LY1:, LY2:)
Royalty Rate: 10%
Advance: $X   payable upon signing
Guarantee: $X   (including the advance) for sales made during the period of LY1 (XXX) through (XXX) $X for sales made during the period of LY1 (XXX) through (XXX)
Payment schedule: $X   on signing $X   (day 1 of LY2) $X   (day 1 of LY2's 7th month)
Territory: United States
Distribution:
Latest In Store:
Sell-off: 90 days
Special Conditions: Licensee must forecast revenue quarterly on forms
Samples: 6 per sku

In accordance with our licensing procedures, the foregoing is a nonbinding proposal only, and is subject to change by either of us. It is intended only to confirm that we have a sufficient level of understanding to warrant proceeding with further negotiations. No binding contract will exist until we have prepared a formal contract, received your signature on it, and signed and returned the contract to you.

Best regards,

Category Manager

Source: © Global Icons LLC

The deal sheet outlines the licensing, the products, the property or brand being licensed, the territory, the royalty rate, the minimum guarantees, channels of distributions, renewals (automatic or otherwise), and any special conditions. Why so many details? To make sure that you and your partner are aligned before moving forward with a full-length contract.

The reason you do it this way is that you don't want to develop a binding document until you've ironed out the terms. If you skip this step, you can end up spending enormously on legal fees—or wasting internal resources—only to find out that you were never in agreement on the terms to begin with.

Don't proceed to the contract stage until you've ironed out terms in a deal memo.

PRODUCT APPROVALS

One of the most important contractual points you should be aware of has to do with product approval, or your control over the licensed product your brand will be associated with. How much power do you have to push back on the licensee? More than you think. But it's your responsibility to speak up if things are heading down a bad path.

Remember: this is *your* equity, your risk as a brand holder. You should exercise all the rights that are available to you, whether in quality, usability, or just plain oversight.

Don't say, "Well, here's the product; they've submitted it; it looks like they've followed our guidelines; everything's fine." As specified in the contract, you should have extensive prerogatives when it comes to approvals and at various stages of product development (3D rendering, first mockup, final preproduction sample, production sample). And don't forget packaging, point of sale, and all the marketing materials.

It's a lot of work, but the devil's in the details. And working with a licensing agency is obviously a big help; they can be your guide and do a lot of the heavy lifting.

PRODUCT TESTING

You should also have the ability—as laid out in your contract—to use, and have the licensee pay for, outside testing. Not everyone is an expert in every type of product; you may well want to have the product verified by an independent party.

If the product is indeed beyond the scope of your expertise—and especially when there's a higher risk to your brand (if the product has a motor or there are safety concerns)—you are completely within your rights to insist on testing.

You should also make sure to get the results directly, so you can involve your own expert, if you're so inclined. Don't just take the licensee's word for it that something is fine and safe when you know nothing about the product yourself.

Finally, pay close attention to the insurance levels on each deal. With higher-risk products that are potentially dangerous, like a snowblower, you must demand (and your contract must stipulate that you have the right to) a much higher tier of liability coverage than you would for, say, a T-shirt.

Above all, don't be afraid to ask for a certificate of insurance. We've taken on many programs where the certificates are out of date, expired, or don't even exist. You'd be amazed at how many people have never even seen their own certificates. Don't make this mistake.

Trust but verify—this is critical in licensing agreements.

AUDITS

Another thing: make sure the "audits" section of your contract is tight. The right to audit your licensee is priceless. Every time we've done an audit for a client, we've had a significant gain, even from world-class, billion-dollar licensees.

Amazingly, many brands don't exercise this right, even though—once again—they have it. As they say, use it or lose it.

Indeed, with any robust licensing program, you should be

auditing your major licensees every five years or so—as a matter of course. Look, they could be the best licensee in the world and still be making honest mistakes. The value of your brand is at stake; you need to treat it as such.

Keep your licensees honest not only with the implied threat of audit, but also with the actual execution of the audit.

DON'T GIVE UP RIGHTS THAT YOU MIGHT NEED

From what I've seen, brands often give up too many rights because they think they don't need them. Say a potential licensee asks for twenty categories, when they're only going to really be able to focus on two core ones. In this case, they end up squatting on those rights, because they never gave the rights back to the brand.

If the rights given to the licensee aren't being maximized, use your "claw-back" or "use-or-lose" rights to have them revert to you.

Also important: make sure the "term" isn't too long. As we saw with Mrs. Fields, signing a perpetual deal is a major no-no. The flip side is when a deal gets renewed automatically; this prevents the licensor from pausing to ask, "Is this really working for me?"

Finally, don't make the mistake of giving up too many territories. Licensees all want worldwide rights, but nobody can actually service the world. Look at your licensee's business plan. See what their proven distribution is and give them rights in those territories only. It's always easier to add territories than it is to take them away.

Never give up rights because you think you won't need them.

WHY LICENSES ARE LIKE MARRIAGES

They say that with contracts in Europe, people care about the *marriage*, whereas in the United States, we care about the *divorce*. I have to admit there's some truth to that. But from a legal perspective, it makes sense. Divorces are what you have to really be concerned about. That's where things go wrong and where you want to be protected. When everything is going well, life is easy and contracts don't matter.

But when things sour, sane people often lose their minds and become contentious. Instead of working through their problems, they fight it out in court. If you ever have to go there, you want to make sure your contract has shielded you well.

Our contracts in the United States tend to be much longer than in other countries. In fact, we recently received a contract from a client of ours in Europe, it was the nicest, friendliest agreement I've ever read. There was no BS legalese. What a breath of fresh air. I was so impressed, I wanted to replicate it stateside, but our attorneys, of course, counseled us otherwise.

For better or worse, when it comes to brand licensing, airtight contracts full of stipulations, clauses, and conditions are a way of life. I wish it weren't so, because at the end of the day, you're either in a healthy relationship or you're not. If it's the latter, then the contract should end and that's that. If it's the former, then you should continue.

Before I fell into the licensing business—as 99 percent of those in our industry have done; there's no clear path to this field in college—I worked as a supplier for McDonald's. They were an amazing customer, for whom we manufactured beef, chicken, and pork around the world.

I bring this up because my old company, which is now over fifty years old, had *no* contract with McDonalds. Deals were all sealed on a handshake. I remember people would ask me, "How can you operate that way? How do you sleep at night?" I would tell them "It's easy: every day I have to make my customer happy. If I don't, they can leave. If I do, they'll stay."

But, alas, that's just not how things work anymore. We

have to have contracts because people don't live up to their word, people change, or the people you shook hands with end up leaving.

At Global Icons, we do use contracts, but if a client is unhappy and we can't fix it, then we can go our separate ways, regardless of what the contract says. And the opposite is also true: if we have a client who's making *us* unhappy or not keeping up their end of the agreement, we'll ask *them* to leave (as we've had to do a few times over the years).

No matter how you feel about contracts, the fact of the matter is that the world of licensing relies on them. It's important that you understand this and do your due diligence. As we've seen, things can and do go wrong all the time, often based on stupid mistakes. Don't let this happen to you.

One last piece of advice when it comes to contracts: time kills all deals. Yes, you want to be vigilant. But you also want a contract that's fair and not too onerous on either side. Ultimately, it's got to work for both parties, and if you end up spending too much time negotiating, it not only sours the relationship but can also kill the deal.

I've seen it happen over and over again. People lose interest and find someone else. Also, let's face it: if they think you are like that now, they're going to always think of you that way.

Like it or not, contracts are unavoidable.

CHAPTER 10

SEEING THE BENEFITS

Just about every company today is using the same marketing playbook: advertising, media relations, product placement, social media, and so on. But you can't continue to grow if you're just doing the same things that your competitors are. You have to look at new marketing tools.

As you know, I advocate "invisible marketing," which means extending your brand into new markets and reaching new consumers through licensing. There's not a shred of doubt in my mind that invisible marketing works. When brand extensions are done right, not only do you get people to try your product in a different way, but you also drive them back to your primary business.

Take our man-cave strategy with Ford. It was an underserved market, and there was a big opportunity not only to fill the hole, but also to really connect with Ford's customers, who loved being in their garages with flooring, toolboxes, wall art, and, of course, hand and power tools.

On top of that, the project built on existing trends: people were spending more and more money on their garages and turning them into fortresses of solitude where they tinker with their car and more. Flash forward, and now a decent size of Ford's program is in a category that never before existed.

These connections are what brand extensions are all about. Look, the money is great. But honestly, that's not the real benefit. What matters is how a licensed product can transform your relationship with customers.

Use invisible marketing to deepen your relationships with consumers.

Invisible marketing has the power to drive customer behavior, shopping habits, and more. Through channel migration, it can move your brand from one place to another, which allows that many more people to discover it.

As we've learned, putting your restaurant brand in a supermarket doesn't affect your restaurant sales. If anything, it lifts those sales, especially when you use coupons to drive back customers.

Does brand licensing *always* work? No. But just because you tried it once and it didn't succeed, don't make the mistake of writing off the entire business. Chances are you did something wrong.

Now you have the chance to try it again using the collective experience of the best and brightest.

CONCLUSION

The whole premise of invisible marketing is simple: all around you, every day, marketing is happening that you don't even realize.

Customers are buying licensed products in droves. Money is being made hand over fist. And it's all happening invisibly.

How are you not taking advantage of this magnificent opportunity? Why are you letting your competitors one-up you?

Brand licensing is a juggernaut—an almost $60-billion-per-year industry. If you're not yet part of it, you're missing out.

It's not too late. Join the party and you too can establish a brand that endures.

ACKNOWLEDGMENTS

First, I want to thank the team at Global Icons around the world, who spent way too many hours helping me with different aspects of this book, from the title to the examples to the artwork.

Special thanks to Bill McClinton, our senior vice president of sales, who had the painful task of being on all my book calls as each chapter was being written, so that we could leverage his wealth of industry knowledge—as well as Mike Gard, our chief operating officer, who made sure I didn't sound too foolish. Anna Steiner, our manager of product development and creative, for her tireless efforts finding all the perfect images for the book. Jonathan Rick, who has helped me write many amazing articles, lent his fine writing skills to the final, painful edit.

I'm also grateful to all the amazing people I interviewed for the book: Nancy Bailey, Kenny Beaupre, Chris Caron, Carolyn Komminsk, Carlos Coroalles, Joe Essa, Henry

Ford III, Kat Cole, Betsy McKelvey, Glen Henricks, and Violet Snyder.

Thank you to Erin Tyler for giving such good recommendations for the book cover and to Michael Nagin for the wonderful design.

Finally, thanks to Donnie McLohon for keeping me on task, and of course Mark Chait, who had to transfer my verbal musings into clear, concise language—you truly rock.

ABOUT THE AUTHOR

JEFF LOTMAN is the driving force behind Global Icons, the world's leading brand-focused agency, with over $5 billion in retail sales. Jeff is a leader in educating executives on the hidden benefits of licensing, and over the years, Global Icons has established a client roster that includes Kleenex, Hostess, Lamborghini, NOKIA, and the United States Postal Service, among others. He is also the owner of Fred Segal, Los Angeles's iconic fashion brand.

Jeff has spoken at many leading industry events, including the Entertainment Marketing Conference, SPLiCE, and the Restaurant Industry Conference. He has also spoken at NYU Stern, UCLA, and USC. He's been profiled by the *New York Times*, the *Los Angeles Times*, CNBC, and FOX, and is a distinguished member of the Licensing Industry Merchandisers' Association and the Licensing Executives Society.

He lives in Los Angeles with his wife and two daughters.

Made in the USA
Columbia, SC
29 July 2020

14940239R00088